THE FIRST AMERICANS

Spirit of the Land and the People

JOSEPHA SHERMAN

SMITHMARK

This edition published in 1996 by
SMITHMARK Publishers,
a division of U.S. Media Holdings, Inc.,
16 East 32nd Street, New York, NY 10016

SMITHMARK books are available for bulk purchase for sales promotion and premium use.
For details write or call the manager of special sales,
SMITHMARK Publishers,
16 East 32nd Street,
New York, NY 10016;
(212) 532–6600.

This book was designed and produced by
Todtri Productions Limited
P.O. Box 572,
New York, NY 10116–0572
FAX: (212) 279–1241

Printed and bound in Singapore

Library of Congress Catalog Card Number 95–072461
ISBN 0–8317–7470–3

Author: Josepha Sherman

Publisher: Robert Tod
Book Designer: Mark Weinberg
Production Coordinator: Heather Weigel
Senior Editor: Edward Douglas
Project Editor: Cynthia Sternau
Associate Editor: Linda Greer
Assistant Editor: Don Kennison
Typesetting: Command–O, NYC

PICTURE CREDITS

Florida Department of Commerce, Tourism Division 30

William B. Folsom 36

F–Stock, Inc.
Steve Bly 22, 81, 114–115
Ken Houseman 42, 43
Mark W. Lisk 20, 120–121
David Stoecklein 68 (top & bottom), 80, 106, 108 (top & bottom), 109

Los Angeles County Museum of Natural History 60

Museum of the American Indian, New York 75 (top), 92 (top), 103 (top)

National Museums of Canada, Canada Museum of Civilization 83 (left & right), 100 (top)

Nawrocki Stock Photo 6 (left), 12, 14–15, 18 (left), 21, 23 (top), 24–25, 27 (top), 28, 29 (left & right),
33, 34 (top & bottom), 35, 48, 49, 52 (top), 55, 56–57, 58 (top & bottom), 61 (left & right), 65 (top & bottom),
93, 95, 96, 97 (top & bottom), 98–99, 100 (bottom), 101, 102, 103 (bottom), 104–105, 107, 110, 111,
112 (top & bottom), 113, 115 (right), 116, 117, 119 (top & bottom), 122, 123 (top & bottom), 124, 125, 126

New England Stock Photo
Carol Christensen 75 (bottom), 77 (bottom)
Michael J. Howell 52 (bottom)
Brenda James 26, 53
Leonard C. Lacue 5
Lou Palmieri 47
Rixon Photography 74
Michael Sheldock 46

Picture Perfect USA
Kit Breen 70, 85
David Schicketanz 13
John Warden 8–9
Stuart Wasserman 82

Chris Roberts 62, 63, 77 (top)

Rockwell Museum, Corning, NY 40–41
James O. Milmoe 31, 59, 118, 127

Tom Stack & Associates
John Cancalosi 37
Thomas Kitchin 10, 51, 66, 67
J. Lotter 32
Lorran Meares 27 (bottom)
Bob Pool 44–45, 64
Bob Winsett 16

Stephen Trimble 6–7, 11, 18–19, 23 (bottom), 38–39, 50, 54, 69,
71, 72–73, 76, 78, 79, 84, 86, 87, 88–89, 90–91, 92 (bottom), 94

CONTENTS

INTRODUCTION

*I*T HAS LONG BEEN BELIEVED *that Native Americans first came to America over the Bering Land Bridge—now the Bering Strait—between twenty thousand and ten thousand years ago. New scholarship, however, places the people of the Pacific Coast and Alaska in America at a much earlier time. Regardless of the date of their arrival, by the end of the eighteenth century the approximately 176,000 square miles that make up the Pacific Coast from Alaska to California supported a population of about 150,000.*

While each tribe had its own dialect and customs, they traded goods with each other and shared a common sign language. Tribes of the Pacific Coast included the Haida, Kwakiutl, Nootka, and Bella Coola of British Columbia; the Salish of Washington; and the Yurok, Hupa, and Modoc of Oregon and California. The Tlingit and Tsimshian lived along the Alaskan coast.

The people of the Southwest may have first settled in this region as long as ten thousand years ago, at the close of the last Ice Age. Radiocarbon dating of a rock shelter on a sandstone cliff in Brazil dates to 32,000 years ago. Some scholars believe that people moved north from South and Central America to what is now the southwestern United States. Others link the Indians of the Southwest to those arriving across the Bering Land Bridge.

The original inhabitants of the Southwest, such as the Hohokam, built such fine irrigation canals that modern Phoenix still uses them. The Anasazis—the Ancient Ones—lived in houses built into the sides of limestone cliffs, shielded from the sun and perhaps an enemy, whose name is now lost. Their descendants, however, continue to live on the ancestral lands: the New Mexican tribes of Acoma, Jemez, Taos, and a dozen other pueblos, and the farming tribes of Arizona, among them the Hopi, Pima, Papago, and Zuni. Some experts believe that the Navajo and Apache are relative newcomers to the region, migrating from the Northwest Territories in Canada sometime around A.D. 1,000.

The harsh landscape of the Great Basin could not support a very large population or a large concentration of people in one place. Still, a good many widely scattered tribes who had similar ways of life, but spoke different languages (or at least different dialects), called the Great Basin home. These tribes included southern branches of the Shoshone and Paiute, who were related through their languages (though they could not understand each other), the Utes, after whom Utah is named, and the Washos.

It has been estimated that during the 1,200-mile journey across the Plateau region, along the Columbia River to the Pacific, a traveler passed through thirty different tribes. The Dalles-Deschutes region, approximately 150 miles inland, still an important salmon-fishing area, shows a clear archaeological history dating back to 9,000 B.C. Successive waves of immigrants brought ever new languages and customs to the Plateau area. By about 1,000 B.C., the ancestors of such tribes as the Bannock, Nez Perce, Northern Shoshone, Walla Walla, and Yakima were already settled in the region.

Many Native Americans would say that they inhabited the Great Plains of North America for as long as the land itself. Archaeological evidence suggests that people may have lived in this part of the country for many thousands of years. More conservative estimates, though, based on the excavation of "sun wheels"—circular sites cut into the permafrost and marked with stone cairns that may have represented the changing of the seasons—place people in the northern reaches of the Plains from Wyoming up into Alberta, Canada, as few as six hundred years ago.

RIGHT: The Wupatki National Monument in Flagstaff, Arizona, preserves several prehistoric pueblos, multi-level dwellings interconnected by ladders.

BELOW: Samoset, a Powhatan Confederacy chief, depicted in an 1892 watercolor by William L. Wells, long after the original Confederacy had been dissolved. The first Powhatan, or Wahunsona-cock, as he called himself, was leader of the Confed-eracy when Jamestown, Virginia, was settled in 1607. It was his daughter, Pocahontas, who married colonist John Rolfe, thus promoting peace between the natives and settlers.

The tribes of the Great Plains have entered American popular culture (in often wildly inaccurate and offen-sive form) as the stereotypical Indian horsemen of book and screen. In actuality, a variety of tribes lived on the immense sweep of the Plains. Iowa, Omaha, and Wichita are named for Native American tribes, and most would recognize the names Blackfoot, Crow, and Pawnee. Other tribes such as the Mandan and Prairie are less well known. The names of some peo-ples, commonly known as the Sioux and Cheyenne, are misnomers attributed to the tribes by French explorers. They called themselves Dakotas, the Native American word for "place of the people of peace."

The peoples of the Great Plains all spoke different languages—though they could communicate through a common sign language—and followed different cus-toms, but they have enough characteristics in common to be classed as Plains Indians. Most, like the Crow and Pawnee, were nomadic hunters who followed the buffalo and lived in easily transported tents called tepees. Other Plains tribes such as the Mandan depended on agriculture and trade with other peoples for their livelihood, and lived in settled villages of bark or earthen houses.

The original peoples of the Northeast Woodlands are believed to have settled there during the first millenni-um, B.C. Before white settlers pushed them off the land, anywhere from one to two million Native Americans—over forty different tribes—inhabited this region. The Huron, the Mohawk, and the ill-fated Mahicans (romanticized by James Fenimore Cooper) all called the woodlands home.

We remember the lands of other tribes with the names of places such as Narragensett, Penobscot, and Tuscarora. At the western edge of the Woodlands, in what is now Wisconsin, the Winnebago tribes were related through language and culture, speaking some dialect of the widespread Native American language known as Algonquian.

Though language and geography separated them, the tribes of the Southeast Woodlands, thought to have settled in the area some time after the first millennium, B.C., shared a number of beliefs and customs. In fact, when the tribes broke up or were destroyed with the arrival of Europeans, members from one tribe could join another tribe without too much difficulty. Some of the better-known tribes of the Southeast Woodlands include the Chicksaw, Cherokee, Creek, Choctaw, and Timuaca. During the eighteenth century, members of the Creek, Oconee, Yamanase—and also runaway black slaves—banded together to create the Seminole of Florida.

ABOVE: A modern couple at the Gathering of Nations Pow Wow in Albuquerque, New Mexico. In earlier times, events such as harvests and hunts provided communal activities for small tribal groups, offering an opportunity for young people to meet and court.

FOLLOWING PAGE:
For the open-sea hunters of the Pacific Coast tribes, the whale had its own spirit, as did the sea, the land, and all living beings.

1 THE PEOPLES

Their Land and Society

BEFORE EUROPEANS SETTLED what is now the Pacific coast of Washington, Oregon, and northern California, the green, wet land was home to several Native American tribes. To the north, indigenous peoples inhabited Alaska, while others to the east made their homes among the snow-capped Cascade Range.

The Pacific Coast Indians' cultures were shaped by the seacoast along which they lived. On the whole, their lifestyles were very similar; it was far easier to depend on the abundant sea for food than to hunt the dense forest, so villages all down the coast were built in sheltered coves, wherever canoes could be safely beached.

Because the sea was full of food for the taking, including such fish as salmon, which could be smoked and stored without danger of spoilage, the village larders were usually full by the end of summer, leaving the tribes with a good deal of spare time in winter. When people don't have to worry about their survival, they have the leisure time to develop an elaborate cultural life, and the Native Americans of the Pacific Coast were no exception. These people lived in a highly organized society, in which every person had a specific role, yet theirs was a communal lifestyle. Each member of the tribe played a part in contributing to the society. Children were the responsibility of all members of the tribe.

Though each tribe had its leaders and respected members such as the shaman or master canoe-builder, the Indians of the Pacific Coast did not identify nobility and commoners in the European sense. Most tribes were matrilineal, tracing their her-

BELOW: This Cree man, dressed in traditional tribal finery and wearing a contemporary version of a Mandan eagle-feathered headdress, poses before a modern-day tepee set up during a celebration in Elmo, Montana.

LEFT: A Haida totem pole, Queen Charlotte Islands, British Columbia. The Haida, a Pacific Coast tribe highly acclaimed for their artwork, carved their totem poles from giant cedar logs. These carvings identify a family's ancestry, much like a coat of arms.

itage through the women of the tribe. They traced their lineage through extended families called clans. In some tribes, careful records were kept to avoid marrying close kin.

NAVAJO AND APACHE

Although the tribes of the Southwest each had their own lifestyles and customs, they can be loosely divided into two major groups: the herders and hunters, and the farmers. The Navajo historically herded sheep and occasionally planted small gardens, and the Apache hunted and gathered food in the tradition of people not truly dependent upon crops. The rest of the southwestern tribes depended mainly on farming for their livelihood, though each relied upon different foods.

The Navajo and Apache, like the tribes of the coast, were matrilineal as well as matrilocal peoples; a bridegroom, for example, went to live with his wife's people. Among the Apache tribes, each nuclear family had its own home amidst those of the wife's extended family, or

RIGHT: The Canyon de Chelly National Monument in Arizona, where seven hundred years ago the Anasazis, or Ancient Ones, built their adobe houses in limestone caves now known as the White House Ruins.

clan. An elder spokeswoman or spokesman led each clan. A tribe in turn was led by a chief or headman, who held his position by ability and charisma. He had limited power; anyone who didn't like his policies was free to walk away. When a special need arose, the tribes would gather together, forming larger bands, but since the population was spread over large areas of the Southwest, they rarely needed formal organizations.

Although the lines are beginning to break down nowadays, there used to be a strong sense among the Navajo of what was man's work and what could only be done by women. The men built hogans and fences and took care of the horses and herded the sheep, and the women kept their homes, did the cooking, and farmed the crops—though a man might help his wife if she was ill or injured. The women also did the weaving, but the men dressed skins and worked with silver.

As with the Navajo, the Apache divided labor between men's work and women's work, but the lines weren't always absolute. The women usually gathered wild plants and seeds, but men joined in the harvesting of agave crowns. Men were the primary hunters of the tribe, but women often participated in rabbit and antelope hunts. Women tanned hides for the family's clothing, yet it was perfectly acceptable for men to help and mend their own clothing. Both men and women made their own tools. Usually only men were trained as warriors, but women often accompanied their husbands on raids. And some women, such as the famous Lozen, who fought beside Geronimo, became warriors in their own right.

RIGHT: A striking stone formation rises from the land in Monument Valley Navajo Tribal Park. Administered by the Navajo, this park, which lies across the Arizona-Utah border, is not a part of the National Park system.

PUEBLO PEOPLES

Southwestern farming communities were organized very differently from those of the hunting and gathering tribes like the Apache and Navajo. Though social life still centered on matrilineal clans, their dependence on agriculture necessitated different customs and ritual tied to the land. Some, such as the Zuni and Hopi, are known as the Pueblo peoples because of the adobe "apartment-house" complexes, or pueblos, in which they lived year-round. Depending on the rain, seasons, and crops for their livelihood, they worked out a far more elaborate code of life than the neighboring hunting peoples.

A Pueblo clan shared a common, and distant, female ancestor. The Clan Mother, usually the oldest woman, headed each one along with her brother, who lived close by. Among the Pueblo tribes, the all-important job of farming was divided into work for men and work for women. The women were guardians of the seed; they inherited valuable seeds from their mothers, and selected the seed to be used for the next season's crop. The home was their domain; a woman owned her house and everything belonging to it, though she was

BELOW: A modern-day Pueblo War Captain in ceremonial dress, San Ildefonso Pueblo, New Mexico. Although much of Native American culture has been lost or destroyed, the pueblos of the Southwest are still active centers for native artists and craftspeople.

LEFT: A Taos Pueblo man dresses in elaborate headdress and face paint for his tribe's Belt Dance.

ABOVE: Wanata, Grand Chief of the Sioux, shown in a lithograph after a painting by Charles Bird King, 1826. Because of their strong resistance to expansion by white settlers, the Sioux were the fiercest warriors of the Plains tribes.

RIGHT: This War Captain looks on at the Feast Day Comanche Dance given at the Tessique Pueblo in New Mexico.

forbidden the world of the kiva, the sacred underground chamber where men worshipped. Men did the actual farming, depending on the uncertain desert rainfall and seepage from the mesas on which the Pueblos sat to water their crops.

Weaving was considered man's work among such Pueblo tribes as the Hopi. Men gathered and carded the cotton, then spun it into thread, although women would dye the thread with bright colors derived from local plants. Pottery and basket making, though, was strictly the province of women.

Other farming groups of the Southwest, such as the semi-nomadic Papago and the Pima tribes of southern Arizona, had a somewhat different form of societal organization. These tribes were patrilineal, tracing their descent through the father's side of the family; a Papago or Pima clan was made up of a male ancestor and his male descendants, and women went to

BELOW: This landscape is typical of the high plateau country inhabited by the Nez Perces and other nomadic Plateau tribes. *View of the Rocky Mountains* (actually the Highwoods, *not* the Rocky Mountains), lithograph after a painting by Karl Bodmer, c. 1834.

LEFT: A Coeur d'Alene man, wearing the ceremonial dress of his tribe. The remaining people of this once large Great Basin tribe live on a single reservation in northern Idaho.

ABOVE: A dignified older woman in ceremonial clothing. Women have traditionally held great power among the Native American tribes, both in decision-making and in economic matters.

live with their husband's relatives. Although the Papago and Pima tribes didn't go to war happily, a village might also have a war leader, known as the "bitter man," a brave warrior-priest who knew the proper spells to insure victory. In addition, a village would almost certainly have a hunting leader, who knew the charms to guarantee enough food for the people.

NOMADIC TRIBES

In the Great Basin, tribal groups were small and semi-nomadic, consisting sometimes of only one family or a few related families. Thus their social structure was less rigid than that of other Native American tribes. Family ties were kept strong by intermarriages. Women held a cherished placed in this society, both as efficient foragers and weavers and as nurturers of the tribe's young. The Great Basin tribes didn't have a rigid hierarchy of leadership, either, though the elders would be turned to for advice.

The Plateau was home to a wide variety of tribes who migrated there from surrounding areas. These people had cultural and linguistic ties to the tribes in the lands all around them, from the Pacific Coast to the Plains and from the subarctic to the Great Basin. This mixture made the Plateau an anthropological melting-pot of customs and cultures.

Though more fertile than the Great Basin, much of the Plateau region was either too high or too arid to support enough vegetation for vast numbers of people living together in any

LEFT: Frederic Remington's painting (1901), shows a brave mounted on horseback. Remington's subjects were drawn from his own life on the Western plains, and are considered to be accurate portrayals of the Old West.

LEFT: Danny Soliz, Ak-chin O'odham, at the O'odham Tash Parade, Casa Grande, Arizona.

FOLLOWING PAGE: Mih-Tutta-Hangkusch, a Mandan village, shown here in an aquatint by Karl Bodmer, c. 1836. The ground on which this village was built was selected for defense, as it was established on a nearly perpendicular bank of solid rock located forty or fifty feet above the river bed.

ABOVE: A modern Seminole man in the Billie Swamp, Big Cypress Reservation, Florida.

one place. As a result, most of the Plateau tribes, like their neighbors to the south, were made up of small, semi-nomadic bands, sometimes little more than extended families. As with the tribes of the Great Basin, such small groups didn't need a rigid social structure. Each Plateau tribe was led by an elder, or advisor, a wise man chosen for the job because the rest of his people respected him. Some of the larger tribal groups, such as the Nez Perce and the Coeur d'Alene, were more strictly organized, staking out their territory and punishing trespassers on their hunting grounds. Other larger tribes such as the Kootenai needed a council of elders to rule on disputes and wrongdoing within the group.

Religion and the organization of the tribe were inseparable to the people of the Great Plains. In their strict social order, ritual was a part of everyday life. Everyone had a specific role to play in the community. Women of the Great Plains were the keepers of sacred knowledge, of theology, healing, and social skills, while men had the responsibility to maintain the tribe through survival skills such as hunting. According to one creation myth, woman was created first to make right choices in the life path, and man was created to be her companion. In this way, women held the primary responsibility for teaching the values of daily life, which were considered sacred. (The first principle: You must assume responsibility for your choices.) Even so, a council of older men, looked up to for their wisdom, governed each tribe. A man or woman could rise to join the ranks of the tribal advisors by brave deeds and wise actions.

SOUTHEASTERN SOCIETIES

The Southeast Woodlands tribes were, almost without exception, matrilineal. As a result, a child was thought of as belonging to the mother, with the mother's brother taking over the role of a male parent. These tribes, too, divided themselves into all-important clans; a person's loyalty was to the clan first and the tribe second.

A council made up of those who had become well known in wartime or in such peaceful activities as healing ruled the southeastern village, though the Clan Mothers also held village authority. The council met to discuss matters of concern to everyone. Any villager could attend and speak at the meetings. Each could vote on major decisions, and the majority ruled.

PEOPLE OF THE WOODLANDS

Most of the Northeast Woodlands tribes were relatively small, some well under a thousand people. The larger tribes were divided into smaller bands, linked by kinship ties. Among such people as the Huron, these bands lived side by side, speaking a common language. Among other tribes, the bands were scattered so widely that people from two different bands might have spoken different dialects. Most of the Woodlands tribes were matrilineal and matrilocal. Each tribe was divided up into clans; members of each clan were related, no matter how distantly, by descent from a common female ancestor.

Women had a good deal of social and political power among the northeastern tribes. For example, though the tribal chiefs were always male, a new chief was always nominated by the Clan Mother, the eldest or wisest woman in the tribe. The candidate would then be elected or rejected by the rest of the tribe. His first duty was to uphold the tribal peace and support the law with the aid of warriors who served as the village police force. The Clan Mother advised him in all these areas.

Late in these tribes' history, just before whites settled in the northeast, the formation of the Iroquois Confederacy proved a notable exception to the Woodlands norm of fortified, separate villages. The land between Lake Erie and the Hudson River Valley, including most of upper New York State, was the territory of five different nations: the Mohawk, Oneida, Onondaga, Cayuga, and Seneca. Up to and during the early 1500s, these five peoples were

ABOVE: A Comanche village in northern Texas, painted by George Catlin in 1832. In the foreground is the wigwam of the chief, and in various parts of the illustration, frames and poles can be seen on which the women are drying meat, and "graining" buffalo robes.

LEFT: Etowah Mounds, a national landmark, comprises a group of prehistoric Indian earthworks located on the river near Cartersville, Georgia. In this view, the lesser mound is seen from the greater mound.

ABOVE: Petalesharo, a Pawnee chief of the Plains tribes, shown in a hand-colored lithograph created from a painting by Charles Bird King, 1821.

ABOVE: Appanoose, a Sauk (or Sac) chief, in 1838. The proud Sauks refused to depart from their tribal homeland after white officials favored settler land claims over their own. This ultimately led to the Black Hawk War of 1832, an event symbolizing the end of the Prairie Algonquin way of life.

LEFT: Oseola, a chief of the Seminole tribes of Florida, shown in a hand-colored lithograph after a painting by an unknown artist. This illustration was originally published in 1838.

constantly at war with each other, in spite of their kinship. But then a man of peace, a Huron named Deganawidah, together with his disciple, Hiawatha (not the hero of Longfellow's famous poem) traveled among the tribes, promoting his vision of a mighty "tree of peace" whose roots were the Five Nations. The confederacy that was formed as a result of his teachings was perhaps the New World's first democracy, complete with an oral constitution and a governing council composed of fifty chiefs, all equal in the eyes of Iroquois law.

The Iroquois Confederacy, sometimes called the League of the Iroquois, created a lasting peace between the five tribes. When the Tuscarora were displaced by European settlers in the Carolinas in the eighteenth century, the Confederacy became six. In the late eighteenth century, their sophisticated government impressed great thinkers like Benjamin Franklin, who wanted to know why fledgling America could not be as well organized.

BELOW: This Seminole family from Florida displays their colorful clothing and some of the tools of everyday life, from the baby's cradle, suspended from the roof, to the churn in the background.

RIGHT: Two small boys learn how to carve a petroglyph, or picture, into the side of a cliff in the Southwest. Native American petroglyphs can still be seen in such southwestern states as Arizona and New Mexico. *Early Picture Makers*, by Eanger Irving Couse, c. 1925.

2 FOOD AND SHELTER

To the original inhabitants of the America's Pacific coast, the land offered an abundant supply of plant and animal life. Warming ocean currents along the coastline produced a mild climate, temperate in summer and with relatively gentle winters.

The people told stories of enormous schools of salmon in the rivers, so many that at spawning time a man could walk across their backs from bank to bank without getting his feet wet. In the ocean, crabs, clams, and mussels offered a seemingly endless supply of food, and herring provided oil as well as food. For those who dared sail on the open sea, whales, seals, and sea lions offered big-game hunting.

On land, flocks of shorebirds gathered at the lakes and streams of the Pacific Coast. The dense forest offered hunting parties scores of game animals, used for fur as well as food. Roots for cooking and healing were gathered in the forest, as well as the edible inner bark of the hemlock. People could harvest a wide variety of berries: huckleberries, cranberries, and strawberries, and local varieties such as salmonberry and salalberries.

BELOW: A grizzly bear is no match for a party of fierce and hungry Sioux hunters, as shown in this Currier & Ives lithograph based on a sketch by George Catlin.

HERDING AND HUNTING

When the Navajo first came into the Southwest they were strictly nomadic hunters, dependent on whatever game they could kill or snare and raiding the settled Pueblos. But when the Spanish entered the region in the sixteenth century, bringing horses, the Navajo diet, along with their unsettled way of life, changed. Pueblo refugees taught them how to grow their own corn, and sheep stolen from the Spanish—during raids conducted on horses also stolen from the Spanish—formed the foundation for a long tradition of sheep herding. The sheep provided the Navajo with a steady diet of meat (supplemented by hunting), and a source of wool.

LEFT: A large salmon catch is cooked in the traditional style of the coastal tribes beside a glowing wood fire at a gathering in Neah Bay, Washington.

RIGHT: The tribes of the Northeast Woodlands could hunt deer, elk, and moose even in winter with the aid of snowshoes which enabled them to pursue their prey even in deep snow.

RIGHT: Stealthily approaching their prey, these Eastern Woodlands hunters have disguised themselves as other animals in order to come within striking distance. A similar technique was employed by the Plains tribes in hunting buffalo.

RIGHT: A Mahican hunter has captured a small animal. Large and small prey were eagerly taken, since they provided food as well as such useful materials as fur, hide, and bone, from which a number of objects could be crafted.

In a region with little water and sparse vegetation, however, sheep need vast areas in which to graze. With the mobility their new mounts gave them, the Navajo became very successful as herders. They could easily allow their sheep the room they needed, and were able to keep up with them. It meant, though, that as the various tribes followed their herds in the never-ending search for grass and water, the Navajo grew more and more widely dispersed over Arizona and New Mexico.

The impact on the Apache tribes wasn't quite so dramatic, but the horse also changed their lives. Until the first horses entered their region, the Apache relied on dogs as beasts of burden. Suddenly, as had happened with the Plains tribes, they were mobile, able to travel swiftly over greater distances.

However, the Apache, unlike the Navajo—although they, too, raided the Spaniards freely—never took up sheep herding, depending instead upon what their men could take in the hunt, from deer and antelope to the smaller animals that even boys could catch. Some of the tribes, like the Lipan Apache, who lived close to the Great Plains, even became buffalo hunters after they obtained horses. All of the Apache supplemented their diets with whatever the women gathered from desert plants.

FARMERS OF THE SOUTHWEST

Life for the Pueblo peoples, as for farmers everywhere, revolved around the harvest. Corn was a vital part of the Pueblo diet, eaten fresh or ground into cornmeal. Among such tribes as the Hopi, cornmeal was the prime ingredient of *piki*, a thin bread which was a staple in the Hopi menu. It could be eaten plain or as an accompaniment to stews. These stews often included vegetables such as squash and beans that were grown by the tribe. Wild foods such as milkweed, watercress, and sagebrush were gathered by the women. Deer, gathered in drives, added welcome meat and provided valuable deerskin, and smaller desert animals such as jackrabbits could also be hunted.

Even though the Papago and Pima lands don't look as though they could support human life, there is food to be had. The fruit of almost every cactus is edible, from the prickly pear, which needs only to have its thorns scraped away, to the cholla, which must be baked for a full day. The saguaro fruit was eaten straight from the cactus, or turned into a sweet jam and drink; the saguaro's seeds were even ground into flour. There were also desert roots to eat, and the flowering stalks of the yucca. As a treat, they made a form of chewing gum out of the juice of the milkweed vine. These tribes also planted some crops: corn, beans, and squash.

Winter was the hunting season for the Papago and Pima, when men went up into the mountains for deer drives. Everyone—

LEFT: A variety of beans, squash, and nuts was harvested by agricultural peoples in many areas. However, it was maize, or Indian corn, grown throughout the Americas, that was the most plentiful food crop for the Native Americans.

BELOW: The Pueblo peoples have been baking bread, traditionally made from ground corn, in outdoor ovens such as these for countless generations.

men, women, and children—hunted desert animals such as rabbits, ground squirrels, mice and rats, and quail and doves.

THE GATHERERS

The lives of the Great Basin tribes were intimately tied to the turn of the seasons. The scarce rainfall and uncertain surface water made farming impossible, and larger game such as antelope rarely entered the region. The tribes of the Basin became master foragers, and learned not to depend on any single source of food. Since an expected crop of pinon nuts or a usually dependable desert pool might fail them at any time, they took advantage of every possible edible plant and animal. What they ate varied with the season.

During the spring, tribes often camped at the edge of a marsh where they would gather edible plants and catch water fowl. Moving onto the rivers, they would then net newly-hatched fish swimming downstream. By full summer, the tribe would move into the hills to gather edible plants and berries as well as rice grass, which they ground into meal.

As autumn approached, the gathering of pinon nuts from small, scrubby pine trees became a communal activity for smaller tribe groups. Later, in the fall, the hunting of

LEFT: Following the ways of his ancestors, Eugene Sekaquaptewa of the Hopi Pueblos tends the Eagle Clan cornfield near Old Oraibi, Arizona.

FOLLOWING PAGE:
Once the Plains tribes began to use horses, they no longer had to depend on the long, laborious tracking of buffalo on foot. *The Great Buffalo Hunt* by William Robinson Leigh.

jackrabbits and other small animals offered the final opportunity to find food in abundance. Winter was harsh on the Great Basin desert, cold and raw, with chill winds sweeping down on the tribes. The gathering of food was nearly done for the year, although men would still hunt small burrowing animals such as ground squirrels, flooding them out or digging them up from their burrows with sticks.

SURVIVING ON THE PLATEAU

Salmon from the Columbia and Fraser rivers and their tributaries was the main staple in the Plateau tribes' diet. Many of the peoples planned their lives around the annual spring running of the salmon, camping near the rivers from May to September, netting and spearing fish or catching them in weirs. The Kootenai took to the water, spearing salmon from their small, lightweight bark canoes. Most of the fish were smoked or sun dried, and some of the dried salmon would be crushed into a powder which could be cooked as cakes or added to stews.

ABOVE: A bowhead whale has been harpooned and brought ashore by a group of Inuit hunters near Barrow, Alaska.

When the amazing rush of fish was over for the year, the tribes of the Plateau migrated to hunt other game such as deer, elk, and caribou as well as smaller animals. The women gathered the all-essential roots, vegetables, and seeds that formed a large part of the Plateau diet. Camas, one of the most important roots, provided a vital source of starch, but the tribes also devoured bitterroot, hazelnuts, and a wide variety of berries including gooseberries, strawberries, and raspberries.

The Northern Shoshone, who lived in a region of the Plateau where deer and elk were rare, traveled east of the Rocky Mountains each year to hunt buffalo on the Great Plains. But hunting big game was no easy matter for any of the tribes in the days before they had horses, when they had only undependable dogs to help them.

The coming of horses to the Great Plains, as in the Southwest, caused a major change in the economy of the region. Their use gave the nomad hunters, with their easy mobility, dominance over the once-superior farming tribes. Those peoples, such as the Mandan, who remained farmers found themselves surrounded by the horsemen, frequently trapped within their village walls. It was an irresistible temptation for tribes like the Cheyenne to abandon their farms, seize some horses, and convert to a nomadic way of life.

THE BUFFALO HUNT

The people who lived on the Great Plains most valued its waving sea of grass for its bountiful game. Here was the perfect environment for one of North America's best-known mammals: the American bison, commonly misnamed the buffalo. They followed the buffalo as the great herds grazed on the prairie grass. This versatile animal was the source of life for these tribes, providing not only food but also the raw materials for most of their crafts.

LEFT: Before being slaughtered, the whale, which supplied an abundance of food, was traditionally thanked for giving its life so that the people might survive.

Buffalo meat was a mainstay of the Plains diet, roasted, stewed, or, in the case of certain choice bits such as the liver, eaten raw. To add flavor, the meat was sometimes cooked over a hickory fire. Whatever meat wasn't eaten immediately was sun dried as jerky or pounded together with berries and fat to make the high-protein, high-energy, lightweight food known as pemmican.

Since the buffalo hunt was of such vital importance to the Plains tribes, it is not surprising that it was begun with ritual prayer and timed carefully to coincide with the annual migration of the herds. Scouts set out first, seeking a herd, judging its size and strength and then bringing the news to the rest of the hunters, who waited downwind so the buffalo wouldn't scent them. During the butchering, a boy who had made his first kill would be honored. He was offered the tongue of his buffalo, considered the tastiest part. In turn, the boy would give

BELOW: The Pacific Northwest tribes often caught salmon in traps, or weirs. Here, two men use dip nets to capture and haul in the fish.

away the tongue, showing his generosity. He wouldn't taste the meat of his buffalo either, as that would have shown greed.

Although the buffalo was the primary source of meat in the Plains tribes' diet, other animals like deer and antelope were hunted as well. Some tribes also ate small game, such as prairie dogs and rabbits, and most included some game birds such as wild turkey and quail in their diets.

OTHER SOURCES OF FOOD

The settled tribes of the Great Plains, like the Mandan, living in their fortified villages along the Missouri, depended more upon agriculture than the hunt. They traded their surplus of cornmeal and beans for finely dressed hides and buffalo robes from the nomadic tribes. The Mandans were good traders, often stripping their nomadic cousins of more trade goods than the nomads had intended.

What the Northeast Woodlands peoples ate, and how they got their food, depended, of course, on their surroundings. Tribes such as the Delaware and Powhatan, who lived on the fertile coastal plains in a relatively mild climate, had easy access to the rich fishing of the Atlantic shore. Once the trees lining the coast were cleared from the fertile soil, the tribes also raised such crops as corn, using seaweed and dead fish to make nitrogen-rich fertilizer. The Montauk tribe of New York's Long Island had another seaside asset: richly populated clam beds. But most of the inland peoples depended as much on agriculture for their food as on any fish or game their hunters could catch.

The highly valued labor of farming was considered women's work by most of the Woodlands tribes. First the men cleared the fields, then the women set to work breaking up the soil with their wooden picks and hoes. They planted such crops as the all-important corn, as well as beans, squash, and sunflowers. Women also gathered wild plants and nuts from the surrounding forest, including mushrooms, fruit, and acorns. Those peoples who lived within easy access of the Great Lakes, like the Chippewa and Menominee, harvested wild rice.

Although a man of the Woodlands tribes might occasionally go fishing alone along one of the many streams, fishing expeditions to the Great Lakes or one of their tributaries were communal affairs, sometimes lasting as long as a month. The fishermen built temporary wood and bark houses for themselves in which to live before returning to their village with their catch of whitefish, trout, or sturgeon. The men fished with their nets or weirs and killed the catch with bone-tipped fish spears.

Hunting was a group effort, too. The Northeast Woodlands tribes hunted game birds, including geese, heron, and turkey, and animals such as beaver and bear. Their main prey, however, was deer. The whitetail deer was as important to the survival of Woodlands culture as the buffalo was to that of the Plains tribes. Its meat fed the people, its hide clothed them, and its bones and hooves were used in handicrafts.

As with the tribes to the north, the Southeast Woodlands men hunted and fished, and the women tended the fields. When a village needed a new field, the men would clear the land and then turn the rest of the work over to the

women, who planted the crops. They were skillful farmers, growing corn and beans together so that the cornstalks would provide support for the clinging bean vines. Two varieties of corn were planted, one quick to mature, one growing more slowly, so that ears would be available throughout the summer and well into the fall. The late-maturing corn was dried and ground into a meal that could be safely stored for use through the winter. The women also gathered wild fruits, vegetables, and forest berries. In addition, bear offered fur and fat rather than meat, and the varied game birds of the southern forests, in particular the wild turkey, were also highly prized.

HOMES AND VILLAGES

A typical Pacific Coast village consisted of up to thirty or more rectangular houses set out in one or two rows in a sheltered cove, far enough back from the sea's edge to avoid flooding. Rarely more than one story tall, they were built of skillfully cut wooden planks and tied together with stout cords. Their front doors and steeply peaked roofs faced the sea. Most had at least twenty feet of private space surrounding them, enough room for canoes to be drawn up and covered with matting to keep the sun from splitting the wood.

Each house was home to a single extended family. A particularly large family unit might consist of up to one hundred people, all of whom lived in a single house. If the family was

ABOVE: A Pawnee
village on the banks
of the Red River, with
its wigwams of thatched
prairie grass, is shown
in this 1832 watercolor
by George Catlin.

wealthy enough, they might be able to afford a house up to six hundred feet long and sixty feet wide.

In the Southwest, most of the Navajo people lived in hogans—round, dome-shaped houses that look something like old-fashioned beehives in profile. A framework of six or eight poles cut from pinon pine, woven together at the top and leaving a smoke hole, supported the structure. The outside was covered with an insulating layer of mud or clay. In regions where wood was scarce, a hogan might have stone walls set in mud mortar.

More than a shelter, the hogan was a sacred home, following the pattern established by the Holy People, powerful supernatural beings. A new hogan was always consecrated. Even today, when most of the people live in "standard" houses, a Navajo family will usually have at least one hogan on its property.

Those branches of the Apache people who lived in the highlands of Arizona built wickiups, windowless homes made of woven poles and brush that look somewhat like the Navajo hogans in profile though lacking the smooth coating of mud or clay. The Apache tribes who inhabited the desert lowlands lived in tepees like their neighbors on the Great Plains.

The Pueblo tribes originally lived on the valley floors of northern Arizona and New Mexico. When the brutal Spanish conquistadors passed through the area during the sixteenth century, the tribes moved, in self-defense, to the flat, easily defended tops of mesas. There they

built rows of adobe houses piled one atop the other. Some, like those of the Hopi, were three stories high, while others were up to five stories tall, with each level connected by ladders. Many of the tribes, such as the Acoma and the Zuni, still live in their ancestral homes today.

TEMPORARY HOMES

The people of the Great Basin, like all nomads, built for mobility, not permanence. A home in warm weather might consist of a simple cone made of willow poles and covered with bundles of reeds, comfortable enough when a family was gathered within around a fire, sheltered from the chill of the night. When the family moved on, they would leave this temporary, easily replaced shelter behind. Winter homes were basically the same, although the reed bundles were thicker, leaving no gaps save for a door and a smoke hole in the roof.

Plateau homes varied from tribe to tribe, and echoed the influence of both the Pacific Coast and the Great Plains peoples. Some of the Northern Shoshone who lived in what is now Idaho had easy access to forests, and built plank houses similar to those of the Pacific Coast tribes. The Northern Shoshone who lived closer to the Great Plains preferred instead the Plains-style tepee. Some Plateau tribes, such as the Kootenai and Nez Perce, used the tepee in the summer but built more permanent longhouses made of a framework of poles covered with woven mats to live in for the rest of the year. Many of the other tribes had two differ-

ABOVE: This lithograph from 1833, after a painting by Karl Bodmer, depicts the interior of the hut of a Mandan Chief, which sheltered animals as well as people.

ABOVE: A modern-day ceremonial teepee at the Jicarilla Apache reservation in New Mexico is silhouetted by the setting sun.

RIGHT: A valuable look at America's past is provided by these modern reconstructions of painted teepees at Canada's Calgary Stampede.

ent types of home as well, digging out earthen lodges with roofs of wood or sod—well-insulated against the cold—for their winter homes, and constructing simple huts of bark, brush, or woven reeds for the summer.

THE TEPEE

The tepee was the perfect home for the nomads of the Plains. Easy to erect or take down, and easy to transport, the tepee's design was based on those of the tribes of the eastern forests, where it was made of a conical framework of poles covered with birchbark or deer hides. The Plains tepees, however, needed a stronger framework than those of the forests to withstand the strong winds of the west.

The bark coverings of the east were replaced on the Plains by the plentiful buffalo hide. Anywhere from six to thirty hides, sewn together carefully with buffalo sinews, made a proper covering. Before a woman could begin work on her tepee, she had to save hides

ABOVE: The teepee, an easily-assembled structure of hides stretched over a framework of wooden poles, was the perfect dwelling for nomadic peoples such as the tribes of the Plains.

and sinew for as long as two years. When she had the hides, her husband provided fourteen to twenty lodge poles; the number of poles varied from region to region, and depended upon the size of the tepee.

Porcupine quills and painted murals covered the tepee, and an inner lining was installed to keep in the warmth. The bare ground, partly covered by the family's sleeping furs or, for the Pawnee and Cheyenne, by mats woven of rushes, served as the floor.

LONGHOUSES AND WIGWAMS

Most of the peoples of the Northeast Woodlands lived in homes called longhouses, an accurate description of their long and narrow shape. Wooden poles tied together provided the framework, which was then covered with sheets of bark. Each had doors at the front and back and a rounded roof with smoke holes at intervals down its length. Sometimes the outer walls were painted in intricate red and black designs. Five or six families, related through blood or marriage, shared each longhouse.

LEFT: At Taos Pueblo in Taos, New Mexico, the native peoples still build their houses stacked one atop the other, just as their ancestors did for hundreds of years.

Porches at both ends of a longhouse held such foods as corn stored in birchbark containers. Inside, families hung their belongings on pegs from the central posts which helped support the roof. Furniture was simple; sleeping platforms lined the walls and served as benches when people were awake, a second tier of platforms higher up provided yet more storage space. Individual families' cooking fires, which burned in a row down the center of the house, provided heat and light.

As on the Great Plains, there were regional variations in the housing styles of the Woodland peoples. For example, some of the more northern tribes, such as the Chippewa and Ottawa, built smaller, dome-shaped, bark-covered wigwams instead of longhouses.

ABOVE: A traditional Seminole chickee dwelling in Florida provides shade from the burning sun and is open on all sides to catch the cooling breezes.

BUILDING FOR DEFENSE

Most Southeast Woodlands people were hunters and farmers, leading settled lives, and, like some of their northern neighbors, they needed protection from their enemies. Wooden palisades as high as sixteen feet surrounded their villages. Sometimes a mixture of mud and grass covered the palisades for additional strength. Within the palisade, homes clustered around a central council house.

Each group of homes included a family's lightweight summer shelter, which was designed to catch every possible breeze, and the more heavily insulated winter house, which had no windows and only one low doorway. Wooden poles provided a rectangular or round frame, protected with woven cane walls covered with clay and grass, and topped with a roof of woven saplings with bark shingles. Though life was communal, a family might also own storage sheds, a granary, and a household garden.

Because of their environment, the Seminole built homes quite different from those of most other Southeast Woodlands tribes. They lived in a hot, swampy area, so they built thatchroofed, open-sided houses, raised on stilts above the damp ground to help keep them dry.

BELOW: A traditional Navajo home, called a hogan, made of a wooden framework covered with mud, stands before Shiprock, an extinct volcano in New Mexico.

RIGHT: This well-protected Secotan village, near North Carolina's Pamlico Sound, was visited by the Raleigh Expedition of 1585, which founded the ill-fated Roanoke Colony.

3 CLOTHING AND CRAFTS

A WIDE VARIETY OF WOOD FIBERS provided Pacific Coast people with clothing, and a weaver could create a variety of water-resistant garments on her half-loom. Shredded cedar bark was used for women's skirts, complete with a belt around the waist. Red cedar bark made water-repellant rain ponchos or cloaks for men and women, which were frequently edged with fur to prevent chafing. Yellow cedar was made into robes so soft they needed no lining, and tightly woven, waterproof rain hats. The creative weaver might dye her fibers or add decorations of ornamental grasses and ferns; she might also include duck down or mountain-goat wool for trimming as well as softness.

Some of the most elegant clothing was crafted from the prized mountain-goat wool, which was difficult for many of the coastal tribes to obtain. The women of the Chilkat tribe, a part of the Tlingit peoples, wove goat wool into colorful, intricately patterned fringed robes and shawls (commonly misnamed "blankets"). The weavers followed designs that were painted on pattern boards. They wove their fabric in panels, which were then sewn together to create the finished robes. Some tribes also wore fur cloaks of bear or sea otter skins. Others, such as the coastal Salish, used a very unusual form of wool: they kept a special breed of small, furry dog specifically for shearing. In the colder regions, such as the Alaskan coastline of the Tlingit tribes, winter garb included long-sleeved deerskin dresses for the women and deerskin trousers for the men.

LEFT: Weaving has historically been women's work among the Navajo. In this photochrome, c. 1900, a Navajo woman weaves a large rug in a traditional pattern.

Both men and women of the Pacific Coast tribes wore jewelry, and the elegance of their ornaments reflected their status. Necklaces, earrings, headbands, and nose rings of local shells, sometimes with bear claws or bits of fish bone added for contrast, were popular items. Traders from southern California brought glistening abalone shell pendants to the northern peoples. Some tribes also used copper ornaments, though these, like most native metals, were rare.

Skin decoration was also popular. In the north, men and women often had their entire bodies covered with intricate tattoos. Tattooing was less popular in the south, though women sometimes had chin tattoos, which were signs of beauty. On holidays, some people wore face and body paint, following the traditional clan designs.

SOUTHWESTERN CLOTHING

When they first entered the Southwest, the Navajo dressed relatively simply. A man wore a breechcloth, leggings, and sandals woven from the yucca plant. Women's clothing was also woven from yucca fibers and included a skirt, leggings, and sandals. Both men and women covered up in woven yucca blankets during the chilly desert nights. The Hopi taught the Navajo "newcomers" the art of weaving cotton and wool, and soon the yucca fabrics were replaced by these more comfortable materials. Women were quick to design attractive mats, cloth rectangles which could be worn as shawls or tied about the waist as wraparound skirts.

When European fashions and materials reached the region, men took to wearing calico shirts and denim trousers. Women dressed in long, wide calico skirts and brightly colored velveteen blouses, often cinched by elegant silver belts. Once the art of silversmithing reached the Navajo, they became experts, producing exquisite necklaces, earrings, and belts studded with local turquoise.

Much of the Apache's clothing was made of buckskin until the introduction of cotton in the late eighteenth and early nineteenth centuries. A man might wear a breechcloth, a loose

BELOW: A Chippewa mother, with her child attached to her back on a cradle board, is warmly dressed against the bitter climate of the Great Lakes region.

LEFT: The clothing of these three Navajos reflects changes in traditional dress brought about by the new materials and fashions introduced by white settlers. Lithograph from an original drawing by H. B. Mollhausen during the Colorado River Expedition of 1857–1858.

RIGHT: A small Plains tribal party, bundled up against the bitter cold, follows a trail through the snow-covered Rocky Mountains. *On the Trail in Winter* by Henry Francois Farny, 1894.

cotton shirt, and moccasins, topped with a cotton turban or headband. A woman's costume consisted of a two-piece buckskin dress made up of skirt and blouse, and moccasins.

Though some of the Pueblo people wore buckskin too, most preferred cool and comfortable cotton clothing in the desert heat. A man's outfit usually consisted of a kilt or full-length cotton pants, a loose cotton shirt, and buckskin moccasins, while a woman wore a belted knee-length cotton dress tied at one shoulder, and moccasins. She might also wear buckskin leggings to protect herself while gathering food from the prickly plants of the desert.

LEFT: In this Currier & Ives lithograph, three styles of dress are shown. From left to right: Osage, Iroquois, and Pawnee.

ABOVE: This early Powhatan warrior wears only a deerskin loincloth and a shell necklace, in keeping with the warm climate of the Virginia coast summer.

FAR LEFT: This Hopi girl, photographed in 1901, has had her hair styled in a "squash blossom," symbolizing that she is ready for marriage.

SEASONAL DRESS

In the height of the summer heat, the people of the Great Basin also wore very little: breechcloths of woven grass for the men and short reed skirts for the women. For cooler weather or chilly nights, women wove pounded sagebrush and cedar bark into sleeveless shirts and pants for the men and blouses and skirts for the women. Winter clothing included rabbit-skin cloaks, painstakingly made from long spirals of fur woven around plant fiber for warmth.

The Plateau peoples' clothing styles closely resembled those of the Plains Indians. Although some of the Plateau tribes did experiment with robes of woven bark, their material of choice was usually buffalo hide or deerskin. A typical man's costume consisted of a breechcloth and leggings supported by a belt, a long shirt reaching to about the hips, and moccasins. A woman wore knee-length leggings, an ankle-length dress held in by a belt, and moccasins. She might also carry a "handbag" of woven bark or grass. Like the Plains tribes, the Plateau people adorned their outfits with fringes and designs, either painted on or embroidered with dyed porcupine quills.

Unlike the Plains tribes, though, both men and women of the Plateau tribes wore woven caps similar to fezzes, often decorated with feathers. In the winter, they wore warmer caps made of ermine fur. Moccasins were stuffed with fur or lined with an extra layer of buffalo or elk hide for added warmth, and people wrapped themselves in blankets of rabbit or groundhog fur and kept their hands warm in rabbit-fur mittens.

ABOVE: These two Ojibwa dancers, resplendent in their face paint, feather headdresses, and beaded costumes, pay homage to the traditions of their ancestors.

RIGHT: At a tribal gathering in Browning, Montana, this Blackfoot man wears an elaborate ceremonial outfit similar to those of his ancestors. The colorful, intricate beading and feathers are typical of the Blackfoot Nation.

The clothing of all the Great Plains tribes was made from soft-tanned buffalo or deer skins. Men generally wore a breechcloth, a loose deerskin shirt, and snug leggings held up by a belt. Women also wore leggings and long deerskin dresses, often cinched by a belt from which hung such everyday tools as a knife and a sewing kit. Women decorated the clothing with leather or hair fringes and lovely needlework of dyed porcupine quills. When contact with white traders made glass beads available, clothing was often adorned with exquisite bead work.

EASTERN STYLES

Deer provided the Northeast Woodlands tribes with most of their clothing, though some of the more northern peoples used moosehide as well. Men generally wore a breechcloth, leggings, and buckskin moccasins, frequently ornamented with paint or dyed porcupine quills. A woman would add a sleeveless overdress, and her clothing, too, would be decorated. In winter, heavier moccasins and leggings were necessary.

Hairstyles among the Woodlands tribes varied widely, particularly among the men, who might sport anything from the traditional "Mohawk" to a shaved scalp painted on one side. Women's hair was long, kept in single or double braids down the back.

Before they had access to silver, Northeast Woodlands people wore shell bracelets, necklaces, and earrings. Shell plaques might hang at women's waists or dangle from their braids.

At a festival, a woman's shell finery might weigh as much as twelve pounds. Feathers were also used in jewelry, and men sometimes wore ruffs of down as well. Headbands of snakeskin or eel skin were popular, too, and people frequently painted themselves in red and black designs for festive or religious occasions.

Living as they did in a warm climate, clothing was not the Southeast Woodlands tribes' first concern. Choctaw and Creek men wore deerskin breechcloths in the summer and shirts, moccasins, and bearskin robes in the winter. Women might wear nothing but deerskin skirts or aprons in the summer, but deerskin dresses, moccasins, and fur robes were donned in winter.

Some tribes, such as the Cherokee, specialized in warm, lightweight wraps and cloaks made of turkey feathers or, for more ceremonial occasions, eagle feathers. Feathers were also worn in headdresses and were made into fans. Tribes living in the humid swamps often wore even less than the other southeastern peoples; the Timuaca of Florida needed little more than brief outfits of animal skins. After the arrival of white men, the Seminole women designed colorful dresses and tunics, patterned loosely after European styles, out of scraps of imported cotton sewn together. Shell and bead necklaces and earrings were popular, and tattooing was a common form of decoration.

ABOVE: A highly stylized representation of the dress of the native peoples of Virginia, shown about the time of the founding of the Jamestown Colony in 1607.

LEFT: The early European explorers were astonished by the near nudity of the native peoples they encountered. In this engraving from Theodor de Bry's *Voyages to America* (1590), a Florida chieftain is shown with his entourage.

FAR LEFT: A woman of the Plateau tribes rides her mount in traditional costume. Women of the Plateau and Plains tribes often owned their own horse herds, and had reputations as shrewd horse traders.

CRAFTS

Since the Pacific Coast tribes lived in the middle of such a densely forested environment, they used wood for just about everything that needed to be built. This included almost all the items used in the home, from cradles, storage boxes, and chests to bowls and spoons. Even the simplest of these everyday objects shows a love and reverence for wood in every smooth, sophisticated line and bit of intricate carving. Red cedar in the north and the redwood in the south were the woods of choice, because they are the easiest to work, but woodcarvers also used other native trees such as the yellow cedar and the alder.

Many creations of the Pacific Coast peoples that are considered art today once served a practical purpose. The baskets, trays, and matting woven by all the tribes are beautiful tributes to the craft. Depending on their intended use—for lightweight storage or heavy household use—baskets were made of spruce roots, cedar bark, or grasses. Weavers added dyed grasses or the shiny black stems of ferns into the weave to make even more attractive patterns. Baskets meant for heavy use were so skillfully and tightly woven that they were waterproof, and could be used as containers for boiling liquids.

THE TOTEM POLE

The totem pole represents the most familiar wooden Pacific Coast object to almost everyone. Though all of them were memorials of a sort, there were several different kinds

ABOVE: This giant Haida totem pole from Vancouver, British Columbia, is typical of the work of these master woodcarvers who endowed their art with the fierce spirit of the land and people.

LEFT: The totem poles of the Pacific Coast tribes are finely carved and painted works of art, as well as powerful spiritual and ancestral figures for peoples past and present.

RIGHT: Though quite different in origin, the painted decoration of this Bannock warrior's hide shield is reminiscent of European heraldry.

RIGHT: Native American beadwork originally employed ground shells to create decorative designs and wampum belts for trading. However, the introduction of glass beads by Europeans allowed an even greater range of design and coloristic possibilities.

RIGHT: The Navajo people are famous around the world for their skill and artistry in making silver and turquoise ornaments, displayed here by a Navajo dancer.

of pole. Used by the Alaskan and British Columbian tribes, when placed before cemeteries, they honored the dead. When set up in front of a village, they celebrated the village's history and protective spirits. When placed in front of a house, the pole reminded everyone of the owner's ancestry. Those who carved the poles were specialists, true artists of the craft.

FAR LEFT: Evening Star, a Green Hawk Cherokee, displays her intricately beaded headband and silver, stone, and beaded jewelry.

TOOLS AND MATERIALS

A Pacific Coast craftsman carried a sophisticated variety of tools: adzes, hammers, drills, and knives, among other gear, with edges and blades of tough shell or stone (often the regional form of jadeite), and points of horn or bone. River and ocean fishermen used a wide assortment of spears and hooks. These ranged from an ingenious harpoon for whale hunting that was made of bone or horn barbs bound to a wooden shaft and glued into place with a coating of pitch, to deceptively simple fishhooks carved or molded from spruce roots.

All of the peoples of the Southwest used stone slabs, called *metates*, for grinding corn or medicines. Precious wood, carefully carved with chert or iron blades, was worked into cradle boards, digging sticks, bows and arrows, and friction drills for starting fires or working jewelry. The Apache also used wood to make a fiddle's bow. A hollow yucca stalk served as the fiddle's sounding board, which had a single rawhide string.

LEFT: The painted rawhide carried by this woman is adorned with a beaded medallion in the center. Her dress is decorated with cowrie shells, which have been used by cultures around the world to indicate status and wealth.

Both the Navajo and the Apache peoples made good use of rawhide for horse ropes and bridles. Rawhide also made a good covering for saddles, which were stuffed with grass and stretched over a wooden frame. Ceremonial shields made of rawhide were stretched over a wooden frame, painted, and ornamented with feathers. Finished leather

FOLLOWING PAGE: Detail of an old Southern Ute belt, worn by a modern chief in a Sun Dance.

and rawhide provided emergency horseshoes, tied over an injured horse's hoofs.

The Lipan Apaches, influenced by the tribes of the Plains, made their baskets out of leather, though the majority of Navajo and Apache peoples preferred woven baskets, which were frequently decorated with bands of color and leather fringes. Carrying straps were sometimes included so that a basket could be easily transported on foot or by horse, and the bottoms of these baskets were often strengthened with rawhide. Water-carrying vessels were covered with pitch to keep them watertight.

EVERYDAY OBJECTS

Perhaps the most famous woven items of the Navajo are the colorful woolen blankets crafted by their women. Although the earliest blankets made in the early nineteenth century bore the simplest of stripes, by the end of that century weavers were tapping into the white market with intricate, elegant geometrics, and even pictorial rugs portraying birds and animals.

Pottery is perhaps the best-known of the Pueblo crafts. Women were the master potters of the Hopi, Zuni, and other Pueblos, and still create exquisite ware of local clays, intricately painted with geometric or representational designs as their ancestors have done for thousands of years.

Basket weaving was another ancient Pueblo art; skilled weavers created everything from serving trays to cradle board frameworks to containers for holding cornmeal.

The tribes of the Great Basin excelled in basket making, weaving containers of grass, reeds, and willow bark—often including different fibers in one basket to create a pleasing two- or three-toned design—that were so tightly made that even the finest flour wouldn't sift through. They also weaved cattail and tulle reed mats to make their homes more comfortable. Twine made from the milkweed plant, chokecherry branches, and twigs could be woven into cradles for babies, which were then covered with precious antelope hide.

Just as house styles varied from tribe to tribe on the Plateau, so did the household crafts. Many Plateau peoples, influenced by the Pacific Coast tribes, were expert weavers and basket makers, working with shredded barks and grasses to create everything from tightly woven cooking vessels and

ABOVE: This cornhusk mask, like those of the Iroquois False Face Societies, was a sacred object reflecting the powers of the earth, and was always treated with great respect.

LEFT: The fine workmanship typical of the crafts from the Northern Woodlands is displayed in this modern ribbonwork basket, made of split ash by Ruth Watso Abenaki of Quebec.

LEFT: The development of coiled baskets and containers made from plant fibers grew out of the increased dependence of the peoples of the Southwest on agriculture. This display at the Southwest Museum in Los Angeles includes a wide variety of sophisticated shapes and patterns.

ABOVE: The rugs and blankets of the Navajos, along with their jewelry, have become world-renowned for their beauty, and both modern and antique examples fetch high prices.

trays to mats for floors and walls, and snowshoes for the heavy snows of Plateau winters. Other tribes, like the northern Kootenai, made snowshoes but not baskets; instead, they traded their clay pots with the Nez Perce and Coeur d'Alene for baskets.

Though evidence shows that some Native Americans did use iron, most Plateau tribes used such easily flaked and sharpened stones as glossy black obsidian or chert, the North American form of flint, for knife blades and arrowheads. They crafted a wide variety of tools from the bones and antlers of deer or buffalo, such as awls, needles, picks, and hide scrapers. The Flathead and Kootenai tribes were famous as makers of elegant, powerful compound bows, made of thin, supple layers of wood or laminated mountain sheep horn. These bows were so highly rated among the Plateau and Plains tribes that the going price for one was a valuable horse.

BUFFALO AND DEER

Every aspect of Plains life from birth to death included some use of the vital buffalo. A Plains baby was first swaddled in a blanket made from the skin of a buffalo calf, and grew up in tepees made of buffalo hide. Hides taken in late autumn, covered with thick, warm winter fur, were transformed into robes and blankets. A particularly thick piece of hide might become the face of a warrior's shield, while extra scraps could be used as the heads of drums. Rawhide strips cut from buffalo hide served whenever good, sturdy rope was needed, or in the manufacture of saddles and bridles. Tails became fly whisks, and hair stuffed pillows, cradle boards, and balls. Horns were turned into drinking vessels or carved into spoons. The buffalo's bones became knives, dice, or useful tools for fleshing yet more buffalo hides, and the buffalo's hoofs and scrotum found a new use as rattles for sacred dances. When a member of the tribe died, the buffalo provided one final gift—the corpse was wrapped in a shroud made from buffalo hide.

Deer were just as vital to the peoples of the Northeast Woodlands as buffalo were to the Plains peoples. Not merely a meat source, dear hide provided clothing and its sinews made the thread to sew that clothing together. Deer bones were turned into awls and needles, amulets and jewelry, and the bright whitetail hair was used in ritual head-dresses. The antlers made excellent digging tools, and were an integral part of a chief's symbolic crown. Not even the hoofs of a deer were wasted—they became pebble-filled rattles.

The Northeast Woodlands peoples wove baskets of reed and corn-leaf mats for floor and door coverings. Clay was also important for the manufacture of elegant pipes, finely polished

LEFT: This beaded vest worn by a Blackfoot man is a sumptuous background for a variety of ceremonial ornaments, of which the most striking is a black claw necklace.

LEFT: A pair of traditional Chippewa beaded moccasins from the Lac du Flambeau Chippewa Museum in Wisconsin.

BELOW: Kokopeli—the flute player—is a symbol of prosperity and happiness who appears on Indian rock drawings as early as A.D. 1000. This large painted jar is a modern interpretation of Kokopeli by Lois Gutierrez de la Cruz of the Santa Clara Pueblo in New Mexico.

and often complete with detailed figures. Though some of the pipes were used purely for pleasure, most were an aspect of religious life.

The members of the Iroquois Confederacy were skillful woodcarvers, using chert blades to create elegant ceremonial bowls and ladles, and intricately ornamented cradle boards. Larger projects, such as cutting down trees, required axes and chisels of harder, less brittle diorite or granite. Chert or bone was used in arrowheads and spear points, and women sewed with needles and awls worked from deer bones.

Shell beads, often crafted for decoration, were also used for wampum. The wampum, strings and strips of beads, was a symbol of the pledged word. Granted as a sign of honor to a worthy man, it was exchanged in marriage contracts or political agreements, preserving the terms of a treaty between tribes or nations. Both a sacred artifact and a means of conveying important messages, wampum is used by the Iroquoi to this day.

RIGHT: This modern Maricopa effigy jar was created by artist Therena Bread. The Maricopas came to Arizona in the 1700s to escape their warlike neighbors in the west.

4 RELIGION AND RITUAL

NATIVE AMERICANS APPEARED TO PERCEIVE the "Great Mystery" of their lives on this earth. The existence of "God" was not questioned; one was simply placed here to follow a life path, an Earth Walk. This was the Great Mystery. All Native American nations have their own stories of creation, of the spirits of the earth, plants, and sea. Each tribe has its own traditions, yet all share some sense of the Great Mystery; all aspects of the physical world were simply manifestations of different spirits.

Storytelling was a tradition common to all Native Americans. It was in this manner that they related histories of the creation and of animals in the natural world. Through storytelling, knowledge and cultural values were passed from one generation to the next.

Living as they did amid the worlds of dense forest, mountain terrain, and restless sea, the Pacific Coast tribes told stories of the spirits with which they were intimately aware—birds, volcanoes, the ocean, and trees. Some spirits were benevolent, or at least indifferent. Others, like the dreadful Cannibal Spirit feared by the Kwakiutl, or the bird-spirit known as Crooked Beak of Heaven, with its love of human flesh, were definitely hostile. These could only be kept at bay through rituals performed by the Shaman's Society.

No matter how varied their individual tribal beliefs might be, one spirit was common to all Pacific Coast peoples. Raven was neither good nor evil, the force that sets things moving and keeps them stirred up. Some myths state that it was Raven himself who created humanity; others that it was he who gave poor, shivering humans fire. All the stories insist that without Raven, life might be a good deal more orderly—but it would also be much less interesting.

ABOVE: A Raven mask from Port Chilkoot, Alaska. The Pacific Coast Kwakiuitl were guarded by fierce entities such as the Raven, who kept away evil spirits.

THE SHAMAN

The shaman—healer, priest, magician—was one of the most important people in any spirit world, and protected the village from angry spirits or the malice of a witch, a man or woman who, it was believed, secretly practiced sorcery to harm or kill an enemy. Shamans also healed the sick through long, intricate rituals of dance, chanting, and sleight of hand. Both men and women could become shamans, though in such southern tribes as the Yurok they were almost always female.

The path was difficult. A would-be healer would fast alone for days at a time, praying for aid and performing ritual dances until, if he or she was fortunate, a spirit helper appeared to set the exhausted fledgling shaman on the proper path.

THE VALUE OF RITUAL

Throughout their lives, Native Americans of the Pacific Coast practiced rituals, from birth and death rites to a hunter's secret, individual ceremony and those associated with the taking of animal life. The first salmon caught each year, for instance, was greeted as an honored guest so that its spirit would feel kindly toward the tribe and send more salmon its way.

The different stages of a person's life were ritualized, too. At birth, the newborn and its parents were secluded for a period so that the necessary rituals to protect the baby could be performed. Though not all tribes practiced true coming-of-age rituals, some ceremonies marked the transition from puberty to adulthood. For most Pacific Coast tribes, death was viewed simply as a transformation of a person's spirit. No two tribes, however, felt the same way about the afterlife. The Tlingit saw it as a pleasant place, but difficult for a human spirit to reach. Others thought that when a person died, his or her spirit stayed near the living to hurry the deceased out of the house by a specially prepared hole in the wall, so that a dangerous spirit wouldn't find its way inside. Funerary rites varied, too. Some tribes suspended their dead from trees, others cremated them. A leader's death, of course, demanded special ritual, often ending in a spectacular potlatch honoring his memory.

THE POTLATCH CEREMONY

The potlatch is perhaps the most well-known, if misunderstood, ceremony of the Pacific Coast tribes. At the ritual, the host gained new status or confirmed his power by giving away signs of his wealth. Yet each tribe saw the ceremony differently. In all cases, the ceremony celebrated not just one person but the entire clan. It could take years to properly prepare for

ABOVE: Priests and healers, the shamans of the Pacific Northwest combined herbal medication with impressive rituals. Here, a Tlingit healer exorcises the evil forces troubling his patient.

ABOVE: A masked shaman addresses the spirits in a ritual gesture. Most tribes believed that certain animals would permit themselves to be slain for food, and that, if the ritual was carried out properly, they would not run from the hunters.

RIGHT: Like many other Native Americans, the Apache mark the passage from childhood to womanhood with rejoicing and ceremony. A young woman at the White River Reservation in Arizona, covered with earth paint, is in the middle of her puberty ritual, which can last up to five days.

FAR RIGHT: A modern-day tribal dancer. During the late nineteenth century, the Sioux, among other Great Plains tribes, performed the powerful Ghost Dance in a desperate attempt to rid their land of the white invaders.

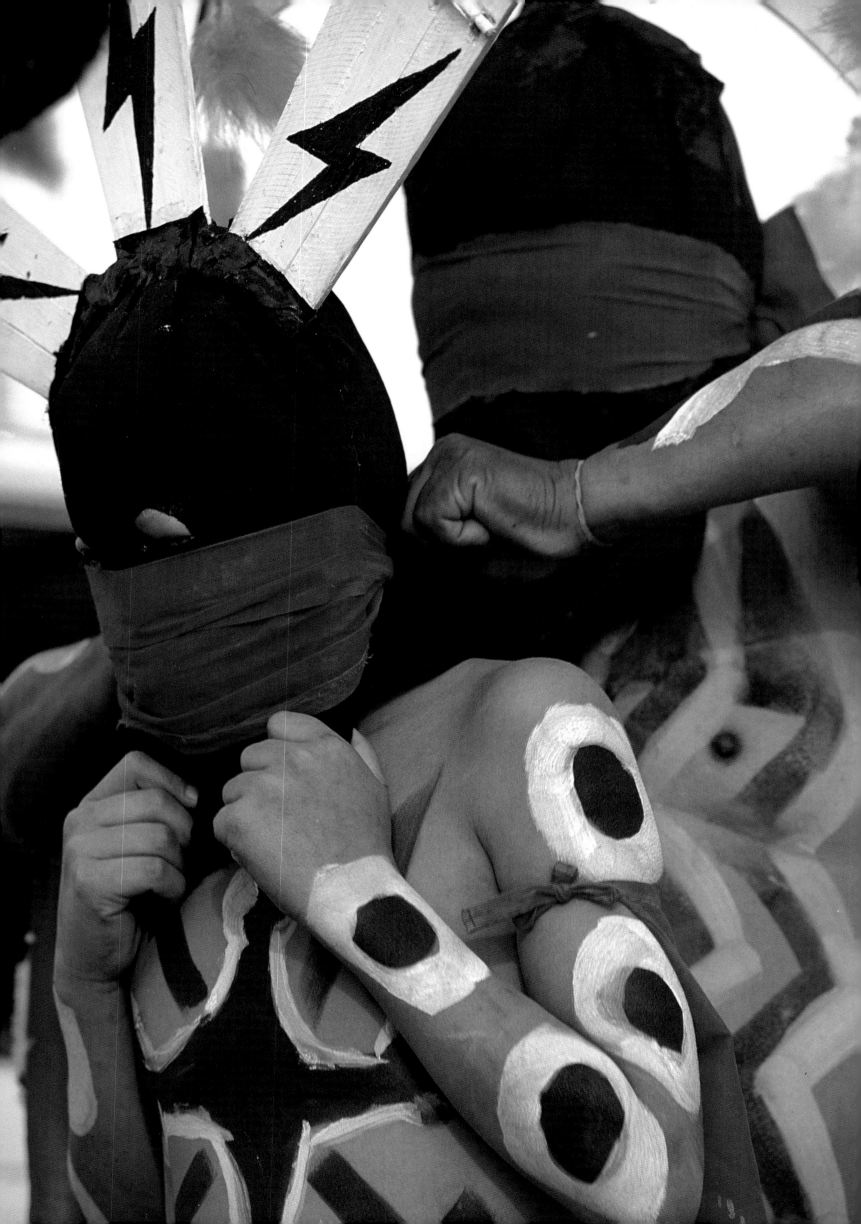

a potlatch, which might involve hundreds of guests for over a week. A suitable gift for every guest, highest to lowest, had to be carefully decided upon, and the proper ceremonial songs and dances rehearsed. Meanwhile, the host of the potlatch underwent spiritual preparation for a full year, ritually bathing each day before dawn, eating sparingly and, in the final days before the ceremony, practicing celibacy.

To the Tlingit, a potlatch might help release a dead chief's spirit from his Earth Walk to his next path. The Tsimshian, too, included a potlatch in their mourning rituals, but for them it gave the new chief the power due him. The Nootka and Kwakiutl used the potlatch to honor the young man who would someday become chief.

The potlatch itself was a spectacular affair, from the arrival of the guests in a flotilla of canoes to the feasting. Songs and dances told of clan myths and family sagas, honoring the living and remembering the dead. Finally, with the distribution of the gifts, the host could claim his true high status, granted to him when his guests accepted the gifts.

NAVAJO AND APACHE BELIEFS

The Navajo of the Southwest believed that the Holy People, powerful supernatural beings, set down the proper path to walk to remain in harmony with this world and that of the supernatur-al forces. In their daily rituals, religion and life's chores were not separated. To help keep to the path, there were songs for every aspect of life.

As a pregnant Navajo woman went into labor, she was sheltered by the Blessing Way song, a chant retelling the way of living in harmony with the land. Her friends untied their hair to help "untie" the baby, and even the family animals might be released to further simplify the birth. Once the baby was born it was anointed with sacred corn pollen, and fed some of the pollen as well.

When a child reached the age of seven, he or she was formally welcomed into the tribe by the Yeibichai ceremony, a short initiation rite which introduced the child to the Holy People of Navajo belief. The arrival of puberty was also a time for ceremony, particularly for a girl, whose new womanhood was celebrated by friends and family in a four-day rite known as Kinalda, at the end of which she was considered an adult, ready to marry.

Among the Navajo, marriage within one's own clan was unthinkable, but there were few other problems for a young woman of marriageable age. She might meet many potential suitors at the tribal ceremonials and dances, and if a young man and woman fell in love, and if their families agreed, he would give her parents a suitable gift of horses, and build a hogan for himself and his new wife within her family's grouping.

In the Navajo supernatural world, spirits had dark sides, too. The *chinde*, malevolent ghosts, waited to destroy those who strayed from the path, and witches brought sickness and even death upon the unwary. Shamans counteracted their evil with elaborate ceremonies that included the sacred Navajo sand paintings.

As with the Navajo, the Apache celebrated when a girl reached puberty. She would be sponsored by an honorable woman of a different clan, and dressed to represent one of the most powerful Apache religious figures, White Shell Woman. In a four-day religious ceremony of dances and chants, the girl would be symbolically invested with the gifts and abilities of womanhood.

KACHINAS AND PUEBLO RITES

Pueblo spiritual life centered on the Kachinas, powerful supernatural beings who protected and brought prosperity to those who honored the old ways; they continue today to be of vital importance to such tribes as the Hopi and Zuni. For half the year, the Kachinas live in their spirit forms in their own lands. But from the time of the winter solstice until the mid-summer Niman Kachina festival, they live in the mortal earth world, dwelling within human bodies, bringing vital gifts such as rain. Pueblos honored the Kachina spirits with Kachina dolls, and ceremonies in which masked dancers impersonated—or embodied—the Kachinas.

LEFT: A young San Juan Pueblo boy, decorated with face paint for the Feast Day Comanche Dance, San Juan Pueblo, New Mexico.

A pregnant Pueblo woman was careful to prepare herself and her baby well in advance by praying daily, keeping her hair and clothing free of knots, and avoiding such taboos as looking at a snake, which might twist the child within her. When the time came for the birth, she would be surrounded by women from her clan, led by her mother, who would help her and pray with her. A symbolic path of cornmeal sprinkled by the father set the new baby correctly on the Road of Life.

Young people of tribes such as the Hopi were permitted, even expected, to experiment with *dumaiyas*, or love-trysts. The only real taboo was that one couldn't love a member of the same clan. Once a boy and girl had decided to wed, the girl went to live in the boy's home for three days, demonstrating her household skills to his mother. Meanwhile, a mock battle took place outside between the boy's female relatives on his father's side and his mother's side, involving much good-natured taunting of the boy and girl. When the three days were up, the young couple prayed to the rising sun together, became husband and wife in the eyes of the tribe, and went to live with the bride's family. Should a marriage not work out, either partner could initiate divorce.

ABOVE: Deer Dancer Kachina dolls. These Hopi Kachina dolls, often given to Hopi children, represent the powerful Kachina Spirits of the Hopi Faith.

RIGHT: The Hopi use feathers in their religious ceremonies to bless objects or to help them ask for divine assistance. A prayer feather has been placed on this *metate*, or grinding stone, to ask a blessing upon it.

RESPECT FOR THE SPIRITS

Everything that existed, the Great Basin tribes believed, was intertwined, part of the super-natural force, the *puha*. Whenever they took something from the earth, whether an animal or a plant, they returned something, even if it was only a pebble. One of the most important rituals of the tribes took place when they gathered to harvest pinon nuts. It included prayers and sacred dances that lasted through the first night of gathering, during which the singers would offer up songs of thanksgiving.

Because the Basin tribes had a less rigid social and religious structure than those of less nomadic peoples, intermarriage was an important way to keep alliances strong. Sometimes a man might wed two sisters, or a brother and sister of one family might marry a sister and brother of another. It was also not uncommon for one woman to have two or more husbands.

Religion among the Plateau tribes wasn't highly structured, and it was considered a private matter. Many of the tribes did believe in a Creator who made the world and everything on it, and who should be revered. Some also believed in an evil opposite, who must never receive prayers. All the Plateau peoples believed in Coyote, the immortal trickster and hero in one, who, they said, had been sent down to Earth to keep things moving and make life easier for people by introducing them to salmon and teaching them to hunt.

ABOVE: A magic pillar erected by the Assiniboin, depicted in a lithograph after a painting by Karl Bodmer, 1833.

ABOVE: A modern dancer performs a buffalo ritual at the San Ildefonso Pueblo in New Mexico.

A child of the Plateau tribes was initiated into ritual even before birth. Then, once a Plateau boy or girl reached puberty, a new set of rituals began, which also included daily bathing and prayers for strength and health. Like the Plains peoples, the tribes of the Plateau believed that Vision Quests were necessary to gain spirit guardians. Both boys and girls went on such quests. Sometimes a child might receive so overwhelmingly powerful a vision that he or she might become a shaman as a result. Shamans among the Plateau tribes weren't sorcerers to be feared, but healers attuned to the spirit and animal world. The tribe would turn to the shaman if the buffalo couldn't be found, so that the shaman might dream and locate the herd for the hunters.

A form of the Plains people's Sun Dance was brought into the Plateau region along with trading goods. Unlike the Plains versions, though, the Plateau Sun Dance involved no self-torture. Instead, a Sun Dance chief would be chosen from the tribe, which was a great honor.

RIGHT: Pehriska-Ruhpa, a Moennitarri warrior, in the costume of the Dog Dance of the Dog Society of the neighboring Mandans. The lithograph is after a painting by Karl Bodmer, 1833.

RITUAL ON THE PLAINS

With their strict social order, the Plains tribes practiced ritual as an integral part of everyday life, and the women were responsible for teaching these sacred values. Woman was created first, one creation myth tells, in order to make the correct choices on the life path; man was made to be her companion.

LEFT: The Sioux Bear Dance, shown in a lithograph by Currier & Ives after a painting by George Catlin, 1832. Catlin wrote of this occasion "They gave us the *beggar's dance*—the *buffalo-dance*—the *bear-dance*—the *eagle-dance*— and [the] *dance of the braves*. This last is peculiarly beautiful and exciting to the feeling in the highest degree."

LEFT: The Sioux Snowshoe Dance, shown in a lithograph by Currier and Ives, after a painting by George Catlin. On the occasion of the falling of the first snow of winter, the Sioux gave thanks to the Great Spirit for the snow, which made it easy for them to hunt game swiftly on their snowshoes.

LEFT: These spiritual entities of the Mandan represent the Sun, the "Lord of Life," and the Moon, the "One Woman Who Never Dies." The lithograph is after a painting by Karl Bodmer, 1833.

Shamans were also important figures in the spiritual life of the Plains
tribes. Not merely healers, they also
helped teach moral behavior to the
young. A shaman was born with his or
her powers, though proper training by
an adult shaman and, in some tribes,
secret rituals as a member of the
Medicine Dance Society, to which
only shamans could belong, were
needed to properly shape that gift.

The most common ritual for reaching these powers is known as the
Vision Quest, in which a person found
an isolated spot and fasted, praying
until a spirit-helper would appear in a
vision to show him or her power-
objects for the medicine bag. The spirit helper would also provide the proper sacred songs and taboos to guide
and help the person through life.

When a boy was considered old
enough—emotionally rather than
merely chronologically—he underwent his first Vision Quest, becoming
a man if he succeeded in receiving a
helpful vision. A girl came of age with
the arrival of menstruation; depending
on her family's wealth and love, she
might be given a feast in her honor.

Although some marriages were
arranged, young men and women of
the Plains tribes often courted each
other, fell in love, and sometimes even
eloped. If a marriage failed, divorce

RIGHT: The Sun Dance, a ritual of
manhood, seen here as performed
by young Sioux warriors in 1874,
was practiced in various forms
by many of the Plains tribes.

ABOVE: Like most people, the Black-foot Nation of the Great Plains had detailed mourning rituals. Bodies rested on scaffolds for the period of mourning, after which they could be interred in the ground.

BELOW: Kiontwogky (Corn Plant), a Seneca chief, depicted in a hand-colored lithograph from 1838, after a painting by F. Bartoli from 1796. The chief of a tribe assumed more than just the physical leadership of his people.

was possible, for both husband and wife, by the simple means of throwing out the other person's belongings. If a man was sufficiently wealthy, he might consider taking a second wife; instead of hating the idea, the first wife was often glad to have another woman to help share her work.

THE SUN DANCE

The most important religious ritual for many of the Plains peoples was the Sun Dance, which honored both the sun and the creative force it represented, and celebrated the courage of the warriors performing it as well. Most of the Plains tribes performed the Sun Dance in a lodge specially built with wood and willow branches for the ritual, but the Sioux danced outdoors. Sun Dancers were almost always young men who had vowed to dance for personal bravery or for the well-being of their families. Painted in sacred colors of blue, yellow, and green, wearing green willow branches at head, wrist, and ankle, each dancer was given a whistle made from eagle bone.

SMOKING THE PEACE PIPE

One way in which a Plains man could salute the supernatural powers was by smoking what we know as a peace pipe with his friends or guests. So serious was this ritual that in some of the tribes no one dared enter or leave a tepee until the smoke was completed. The ritual was begun by the man hosting the smoke, ceremonially pointing the pipe stem to the sky, the ground, and the four directions, saying as he did, "Spirit Above, smoke." Then he would pray for spiritual help for those within the tepee, smoke the pipe, then pass it around, from right to left, with the sun.

Peace pipes were also smoked on the return of a war or hunting party, in order to cleanse the men after the taking of a life, animal or human. The contents of the pipe varied; the southern tribes used a mixture of sumac and tobacco, while the northern tribes preferred red willow bark and tobacco.

POWERS IN THE WOODLANDS

The world of the Northeast Woodlands tribes teemed with powerful spirits, present in earth, forest, and sky. The tribes of the Iroquois Confederacy believed that humanity began when Sky-Woman, impregnated by the Earth Holder, fell to Earth, where she gave birth to Great Spirit and Evil Spirit. After her death, Great Spirit turned her head into the sun and her body into the moon and stars, then went on to create life on Earth. Her brother, Evil Spirit, was banished to the netherworld, but continues to try to harm Great Spirit's creations.

One of the most familiar religious organizations to outsiders is the False Face Society, which was a healing society whose members wore sacred masks representing the mercurial and sometimes dangerous forces that could be used for curing the sick. So sacred

and powerful were these masks that one was never left face up, nor could one be placed on public display.

The Northeast Woodlands peoples also had four types of highly respected shaman: those who could affect the weather, those who could predict the future, those who were healers, and those who could find lost objects.

Children were cherished by the Woodlands tribes. Female babies were especially welcome, both because they continued the matrilineal line of the clan's decent and as potential child-bearers themselves. Among the Iroquois nations, the Clan Mother usually named the tribe's babies, but other Woodlands tribes hired professional namers, who acted more or less as god-parents. Later, the growing young man or woman would receive an adult name through deeds or visions.

RITUALS AND TABOOS

Although there were taboos concerning marriage, particularly the one forbidding two members of the same clan to wed, courtship and marriage among the Woodlands tribes was not quite a formalized affair. Properly, a boy's family arranged the whole matter of finding him a suitable bride; but while the parents suggested mates, the young people often did their own choosing.

ABOVE: In this Mandan hunting ritual painted by George Catlin, Buffalo Dancers honor and sum-mon the sacred animals. They wear buffalo skins and imitate the animals' move-ments in order to bring their spirits closer for the hunters.

Ritual surrounded the end of a Northern Woodlands person's life on Earth. When a member of the family died, he or she was dressed in his or her finest clothing and ornaments. The body was taken out through the western wall of the house, in the direction of the land of the dead. Some of the tribes buried their dead directly in the ground, with ceremonies depending on the deceased person's clan and rank. The Huron first interred their dead in coffins raised on poles. After ten to twelve years, the bones were taken down and buried in communal pit.

Many other ceremonies, celebrated with ritual dancing and feasting, were held throughout the Woodlands year. The Green Corn Festival, in late summer, was a particularly important thanksgiving rite which celebrated the gift of corn. The Iroquois Ceremonial of Midwinter was perhaps even more important. A solstice celebration taking place for a week, it brought in the New Year through days of solemn rituals and dancing.

WOODLAND SPIRITS

Religion was closely related to government among the Southeast Woodlands tribes. A council member was dedicated in childhood, and underwent much of the same training of a young shaman or medicine man. A medicine man was an honored member of the tribe. In addition to serving as a priest, he was often a skilled healer with a wide range of effective herbal medicines, many of which are being studied by scientists today.

The tribes of the southeast believed that woodland spirits hid among the trees. They also believed in a supreme deity, a three-fold god so sacred the name was not spoken aloud. The sun and the moon protected the people and gave them fire. In addition, there were other important supernatural beings, such as those who symbolized the four directions: North or Defeat, West or Death, South or Peace, and East or Power in War. Most rituals revolved around the seasons, celebrating the first new moon of spring, the ripening of the new corn crop, or the season's harvest.

All the Southeast Woodlands tribes celebrated Busk, the autumn harvest festival, as their most sacred holiday. On the first day, the women cleaned and swept the family homes while the men took care of the council house. All fires, including the sacred fires burning in the council house, were extinguished. On the second and third days the people fasted. On the fourth day, they held a great feast and the tribe's shaman lit a ceremonial fire from which all the family fires could be relit. The shaman roasted ears of corn in the ceremonial fire; the new year had begun.

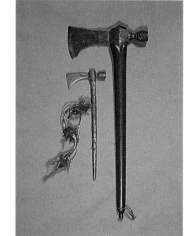

LEFT: The sacred smoking of a ritual pipe is common to many Native American tribes. These Blackfoot pipes are elaborately carved and decorated.

FAR LEFT: A Choctaw ballplayer, in a painting by George Catlin, 1844. These players hold a stick in each hand, and by leaping into the air, they must catch the ball and throw it, without either striking it or catching it in their hands.

FOLLOWING PAGE: The Choctaw Ball-Play Dance, in a painting by George Catlin, 1844. The evening before this ritual game, each party of players assembled by torchlight in their special dress and danced for a quarter of an hour, rattling their ball sticks, and singing loudly to the Great Spirit for his favor in the outcome of the game.

LEFT: The Mandan Green Corn Dance, depicted in a painting by George Catlin, 1832. The harvest time for green corn, considered a luxury by all the tribes who cultivated it, was the occasion for a celebration of thanksgiving that included sacrifices, dancing, and singing.

5 TRADING, WARFARE, AND THE WHITE MAN

CONTACT WITH THE WHITE MAN, beginning during the eighteenth century, spelled the beginning of the end of an era in Native American history, bringing disease and eventually the erosion of tribal culture, as whites sought to "civilize" a culture that was thousands of years old.

The ever-increasing trading contacts introduced devastating European diseases such as smallpox, to which the native population had no resistance. The arrival of white settlers, administrators, and missionaries in Washington and Oregon during the mid-nineteenth century resulted in the forced removal of some tribes from their ancestral grounds to reservations far from the coast. The new government banned such age-old customs as the potlatch.

Further south, the Spanish invaded California during the eighteenth century, bringing missionaries with them that abruptly altered the tribal way of life. The new rulers forced Native Americans into the role of docile servants, outlawing their tribal practices and forcing Christianity upon them.

When a new wave of settlers and gold seekers swept over nineteenth-century California, those Native Americans who survived brutality and outright massacre were forced onto barren reservations. A way of life—and very nearly a people— ended with the arrival of white towns and cities. However, many of the tribes managed to maintain their customs in secret. They could sidestep the potlatch ban, for example, by simply calling the ceremony a "party."

BELOW: William Penn's peace treaty with the native peoples established early on their friendly relationship with the Quakers who settled in the province of Pennsylvania, formally chartered by King Charles II of England in 1681.

WARRIORS AND HUNTERS

The Spanish were the first whites to invade the Southwest. In some ways, Navajo and Apache life changed for the better with the early invasion, providing them with horses

LEFT: A modern-day Shoshone-Bannock man, astride his horse, carries the arms and wears the traditional battle dress of his tribe.

RIGHT: This photograph is part of a live-action battle sequence staged by Shoshone-Bannock men for a photographer whose work was used to publicize Native American activities in Idaho.

RIGHT: In this reenactment of a warrior charging into battle, one can feel the fierce determination of the native peoples in defending their tribal lands.

RIGHT: The introduction of the horse to North America dramatically altered the nature and strategies of warfare for the native peoples, both among themselves and in their actions against the invasions of the white settlers.

and, in the case of the Navajo, sheep and a profitable new business. Later, the invasion of the other Europeans and Americans pushed them onto small reservations. In 1846, the United States took possession of New Mexico and Arizona, building heavily armed garrisons on Navajo soil to oversee a never-ending stream of California-bound gold seekers who helped themselves to Navajo game.

The Navajo fought back in a series of bloody raids against the invaders and the United States army. Theses bat-

ABOVE: In this early engraving (c. 1591), the Timucua of Florida are shown attacking a settler fortress in a dramatic night battle.

tles on the government frontier continued through the years of the Civil War until, in 1862, it seemed as though the Navajo would be completely destroyed. Under the command of Colonel Christopher "Kit" Carson a combination of superior arms, a scorched-earth policy, and psychological warfare defeated the Navajo and eroded their culture. At the end of the struggle, United States' forces held eight thousand Navajos captive.

Though it was an expensive victory for the United States, which now promised to care for the Navajo, they signed a treaty in 1868, giving the Navajo a 3.5 million-acre reservation in northeastern Arizona and northwestern New Mexico. When they returned to their homeland, it had been devastated by the years of war. Later, the government broke its promise when building the Santa Fe Railroad in the 1880s. Even so, the Navajos have survived and continue to travel along the path first set out for them by the Holy People.

As with the Navajos, the warrior Apaches fought back against the United States army in a protracted series of battles that produced such leaders as the famous Chiracahua Apache, Cochise. The Apache also lost to superior weaponry. In 1873, Apache bands were forced onto the San Carlos Reservation in Arizona. Although the war leader known as Geronimo continued to fight back until 1886, the old days of the warriors were numbered.

Today, the majority of Apaches live on adjoining reservations, San Carlos and Fort Apache, where they have become accomplished cattlemen. Like the Navajo, many of the Apache people today proudly keep alive the memories and time-honored ways of their ancestors.

CONQUISTADORS AND SETTLERS

The Pueblo tribes, being farmers, were primarily involved with their crops, though they could and did fight fiercely when the Spaniards tried to conquer them. While some of the

LEFT: Tecumseh, as leader of a tribal alliance, was defeated by General William Henry Harrison at Tippecanoe in 1811. When the men faced each other again two years later at the battle of the Thames River in Ontario, Tecumseh fell and the struggle of his people ended.

RIGHT: Both the men and women of the Comanches, the "Lords of the Southern Plains," were exceptionally skilled on horseback, and Comanche mounted warriors defeated the Texas Rangers in several territorial battles during the 1830s.

BELOW: The May 2, 1868 issue of *Harper's Weekly* contained this illustration showing Sioux warriors preparing to attack peaceful settlers. It was usual at the time to portray "Indians" as fierce savages, and to ignore the white man's treatment of them.

tribes were decimated, others, like the Hopi, impregnable in their adobe fortresses, held off the invaders so successfully that by 1680, the year of the Pueblo Revolt, they had driven them away forever. The Hopi so totally shut out any Spanish influence that they have refused to become Christianized and practice their own faith to this day.

The California gold rush spelled the downfall for the tribal way of life in the Great Basin. Though the first gold diggers had little impact, they were closely followed by hordes of settlers. The discovery of gold and silver in Nevada brought a new rush into the region, and with it a devastating blow to the fragile Great Basin ecology. White settlers cut down the precious pine trees, and their horses and cattle destroyed the grasses. Diseases such as cholera decimated the tribes, and the survivors found themselves pushed onto reservations after the United States government laid claim to the region.

PLATEAU TRADING

Crossed by such broad waterways as the Columbia and Fraser Rivers, the Plateau was the center of a thriving trade between the people who lived near the rivers and those of the Pacific Coast. The coming of the horse had an enormous affect on trading. Now the Plateau tribes did not have to depend on the coastal canoes to bring goods to them. With horses they could trade widely on their own, going into California and the Great Plains,

BELOW: "You have driven away our game and our means of livelihood out of the country, until now we have nothing left that is valuable except the hills that you ask us to give you . . . ." —WHITE GHOST. *War Dance of the Sioux* from a painting by Rudolf Cronau.

ABOVE: Not all explorers were met with hostility, as is illustrated by George Catlin's 1832 painting of the great hospitality shown to him by Mahtotohpa (Four Bears), chief of the Mandans, who threw a feast in his own lodge for the traveling artist.

communicating with the sign language known throughout most of the West.

One of the first white men to explore the Plateau was a Yankee sea captain named Robert Gray, who in 1792 sailed up the Columbia River—named by him after his ship—into what would later become the Oregon territory. Then the Lewis and Clark expedition of 1804 to 1806 marked the first true hint of major changes to come to the Plateau tribes, as the government of the young United States began to realize the region's economic potential. The years immediately following the expedition saw an influx of whites and a sudden surge in trade between the newcomers and the Plateau tribes. Tragically, the white traders brought diseases here, too, and nearly exterminated the entire Chinook people.

A decade later, the white traders were replaced by a wave of settlers, heading by the thousands towards the rich land of Oregon over the newly opened Oregon Trail. As towns sprang up and expansion continued, Plateau tribal lands were imperiled, and then, acre by acre, lost through treacherous treaties. The peoples of the Plateau fought

LEFT: A modern Shoshone-Bannock man in traditional warrior dress demonstrates the role of the foot scout.

LEFT: First wagon trains, and then railroads increased native peoples' fears of a never-ending invasion of white settlers. Here, a war-party attacks a stagecoach of the Overland Express in Utah in 1862.

RIGHT: Tecumseh, the great Shawnee leader, tried to unite all Native American peoples into an alliance to defend their lands. His death in 1813 brought an end to this league of tribes.

back in several bloody battles, but they were outnumbered and confronted too often by the better-armed United States soldiers.

Any hope of success the Plateau tribes might have had was further complicated by the presence of well-meaning missionaries who, by the middle of the nineteenth century, had Christianized half of the Nez Perce, permanently dividing the tribe. The Christianized Nez Perce signed a treaty ceding their tribal lands, but the rest of the Nez Perce rejected the treaty. Led by the heroic Chief Joseph, they fought bravely, carrying on a running battle with the United States cavalry northward for long, weary miles. In 1877, they were trapped by the soldiers only thirty miles from Canadian sanctuary, and forced, as were most of the Plateau tribes, onto reservations.

RAIDING AND COMBAT

Horse raiding on other tribes was raised to a fine art among the peoples of the Great Plains. Outright warfare was just as dangerous as raiding. Whether the tribes dueled over honor or the right to hunt buffalo on certain lands, a full-fledged battle was much easier to wage from horseback. Early warriors fighting on foot had used a large, bulky shield and awkward rawhide armor, but a mounted warrior needed only a small shield and bow and could discard his armor in favor of speed, charging down on a foe to fight him hand to hand.

In the Woodlands of the northeast, a war raid started with the choosing of a war chief, a warrior skilled in battle who had been granted a dream or vision of success. Those who

LEFT: Mandan archers began their training at an early age, when village boys between the ages of seven and fifteen would fight mock battles with blows and blunt arrows under the charge of experienced warriors.

LEFT: American forts such as this one provided stationary targets which were frequently the object of attack by native peoples. Here, Fort McKenzie is shown under siege in an 1833 lithograph after a painting by Karl Bodmer.

LEFT: The tribes of the Great Plains communicated across the vast distances of the region with carefully controlled smoke from signal fires in a form of shorthand. *The Smoke Signal* by John Mix Stanley (1868).

FOLLOWING PAGE:
The young warrior leader beside a venerable tribal chief brings to mind the roles and relationships of Crazy Horse and Sitting Bull as they met General Custer at Little Bighorn in 1876.

wished to join him on the raid would show their acceptance of him by smoking a sacred pipe of tobacco, then gathering at his longhouse for a feast and a planning session. The war bundle, which contained objects sacred to individual warriors, was honored and prepared for carrying on the upcoming raid.

Warriors armed themselves with bows and arrows or clubs. Though raiders often couldn't afford to slow themselves down with so much extra weight, they sometimes wore arrow-resistant armor of wooden strips laced tightly together and carried large shields of cedar bark.

The point of a raid was to get into an enemy village and do as much quick damage and gain as much personal honor through the killing of a foe as possible before leaving. Scalp-taking was common among the other Northeast Woodlands peoples.

ALLIES OF THE IROQUOIS CONFEDERACY

BELOW: Frederic Remington's painting of this native scout captures the spirit of the lone horsemen who watched over the land for intruders and enemies.

The first Europeans to arrive in North America early in the seventeenth century came to the Northeast Woodlands as traders. The French eventually settled what would become Quebec, while the English and some of the Dutch populated the lands further south. At first, relations with the tribes were peaceful; the Europeans exchanged metal goods for the tribes' knowledge of the land. But the peace couldn't last.

The Iroquois Confederacy used its newly gained European firearms to nearly wipe out their Huron enemy in 1649, making itself the dominant Woodlands force for nearly half a century. Meanwhile, the number of European settlers steadily increased, as did their demand for more land. In Virginia, the local tribes had already fought for and lost their home to the English. The pattern would repeat itself further north.

The tribes also became involved in wars between Europeans on Native American soil. First, the Iroquois Confederacy fought with the British against France. Then the Revolutionary War broke out between the colonies and England. The Iroquois, allies of the English, suffered a defeat at American hands that destroyed them as a power. Soon the other tribes would face defeat of a different sort as they, like the southern tribes, were forced from their lands.

WAR AND DEFEAT

There were often feuds between the various clans of the Southeast Woodlands, and sometimes these feuds would spill out from one village to engulf two tribes in

LEFT: "I want to know what you are doing on this road. You scare all the buffalo away. I want to hunt in this place. I want you to turn back from here. If you don't, I will fight you again."—SITTING BULL

BELOW: The Fetterman Massacre, during which Captain William Fetterman's eighty-man reserve cavalry unit was ambushed by 1,500 hidden native warriors in 1866, at the time of the Red Cloud War.

genuine warfare. Surprise was the southeastern warriors' favorite tactic; if a band was discovered before it could attack, it might very well retreat without striking a blow. Unlike the swift raids of the Plains tribes, where the primary objective was the counting of coup, the Southeast Woodlands people's battles were fierce and deadly, often resulting in the taking of scalps or even the killing of all the enemy. The fate of any enemies unlucky enough to be taken captive rested, as in the north, in the hands of the women.

The arrival of Spanish explorers in the sixteenth century radically changed the lives of the Southeast Woodlands tribes, and meant the end for many of them. The newcomers, armed with deadly firearms and steel weapons, thought nothing of destroying any who stood in their way. They brought European diseases here, too, which wiped out entire Indian villages. Before the tribes could recover from this first wave of destruction, the French and British started fighting over their lands. The Europeans had taken control of the lands, fighting their wars, trapping, and farming.

By 1710, the European quest for slaves had virtually destroyed the tribes of northern Florida. The Indian survivors, together with runaway black slaves, joined together in the southeastern swamp land to form a new people, the Seminole. Though most Seminole were exiled by the new United States government, others held out for years in the Florida swamps, waging guerrilla warfare until at last they won; their descendants still occupy their lands, and have successfully sued the United States government for restitution and lands.

LEFT: Geronimo, leader of the Apaches, who surrendered with his forces to General Nelson Miles in 1886, ending the Apache Wars.

BELOW: General Custer's last stand at the battle of Little Bighorn, Montana, in 1876. Custer's forces were decimated by Sitting Bull, chief of the Hunkpapa Sioux, and Custer himself died on the battlefield during his surprise attack on the Sioux.

ABOVE: In 1890, by coincidence also the year of the Sioux massacre at Wounded Knee, the United States Census Bureau declared that there was no longer a line of frontier settlement in the West. It was the end of a long struggle between the white settlers and the native peoples, and the cost—and loss—was incalculable for both sides.

RIGHT: This proud Plains warrior raises his arm in a gesture of peace. Although the artist has painted him with his right armed raised, the traditional peace sign was made by raising the left arm, closest to the heart. *The Sign of Peace* by Henry Francois Farny (1908).

THE TRAIL OF TEARS

Other tribes were not so fortunate. As the new American nation grew, it demanded more and more southern land to produce cotton. Soon the state governments insisted on the removal of the native peoples, who were already outnumbered by the white settlers and considered to be uncivilized "heathens," not worthy of the land they held. Even though the Five Civilized Tribes—the Cherokee, Choctaw, Chickasaw, Creek, and Seminole—had long since incorporated Christianity into their religious rituals, they had no choice. In 1830, the government forcibly relocated the Choctaw to Oklahoma on a harsh winter march that saw more than a quarter of the unwilling emigrants succumbing to hunger or sheer exhaustion.

Between 1834 and 1838, the Creek, Cherokees, and Chickasaws followed them in what was to become known as the Trail of Tears. Exiled to Oklahoma, the Creek took with them the last Native spirit from the southern lands east of the Mississippi. America pushed west to Texas and the Great Plains. But a small remnant of the Cherokee nation did, like the Seminole, manage to hold onto at least part of its land by obtaining United States citizenship, which exempted them from being ousted. (However, most Native Americans were not considered citizens until an act of Congress in 1924.) Today, descendants of those Cherokee occupy legally purchased reservation lands in North Carolina. They continue to use the written language devised by the brilliant Sequoyah in the early nineteenth century, and keep the customs of their ancestors.

INDEX